The PARADOX
of JAMESTOWN

1585–1700

★ ★ *The Drama of* AMERICAN HISTORY ★ ★

The PARADOX
of JAMESTOWN

1585–1700

Christopher Collier
James Lincoln Collier

Benchmark Books

MARSHALL CAVENDISH
NEW YORK

ACKNOWLEDGMENT: The authors wish to thank Martin H. Quitt, Dean of Graduate Studies and Professor of History, University of Massachusetts at Boston, for his careful reading of the text of this volume of The Drama of American History, and his thoughtful and useful comments. The work has been much improved by Professor Quitt's notes. The authors are deeply in his debt but, of course, assume full responsibility for the substance of the work, including any errors that may appear.

Photo research by James Lincoln Collier
Cover photo: *Jamestown-Yorktown Foundation*

PICTURE CREDITS: The photographs in this book are used by permission and through the courtesy of: *Corbis-Bettmann*: 11 (left), 11 (right), 12, 18, 19, 22, 23, 25 (left), 25 (right), 28, 30, 48, 52, 56, 57. *UPI/Corbis-Bettmann*: 15, 16. *Jamestown-Yorktown Educational Trust*: 33, 36, 37 (left), 38, 39, 40, 44, 50, 51, 58, 62, 63, 64, 65, 67 (top), 67 (bottom), 68, 70. *Colonial Williamsburg Foundation*: 37 (right), 75, 77, 81, 82.

AUTHORS' NOTE: The human beings who first peopled what we now call the Americas have traditionally been called *Indians*, because the first Europeans who landed in the Americas thought they had reached India. The term *Indians* is therefore not very accurate, and other terms have been used: *Amerinds*, and more recently, *Native Americans*. The Indians had no collective term for themselves. Today, most of them refer to themselves as Indians, and we will use that term here, while understanding that it is not very accurate.

Benchmark Books
Marshall Cavendish Corporation
99 White Plains Road
Tarrytown, New York 10591-9001

Library of Congress Cataloging-in-Publication Data

Collier, Christopher, date
The paradox of Jamestown, 1585-1700 /
Christopher Collier and James Lincoln Collier.
p.   cm. — (The drama of American History)
Summary: Discusses the circumstances surrounding English colonization of Virginia
and the evolution of slavery in that colony.
ISBN 0-7614-0437-6 (lib. bdg.)
1. Jamestown (Va.)—History—Juvenile literature. 2. Virginia—History—Colonial period,
ca. 1600-1775—Juvenile literature. 3. Slavery—Virginia—Jamestown—Juvenile literature.
[1. Virginia—History—Colonial period, ca. 1600-1775. 2. United States—History—Colonial
period, ca. 1600-1775. 3. Slavery—Virginia.] I. Collier, James Lincoln, date. II. Title.
III. Series: Collier, Christopher, date Drama of American history.
F234.J3C65   1998   96-34998
975.5'4251—dc20   CIP
                                                                AC
Printed in the United States of America

1   3   5   6   4   2

CONTENTS

PREFACE

Over many years of both teaching and writing for students at all levels, from grammar school to graduate school, it has been borne in on us that many, if not most, American history textbooks suffer from trying to include everything of any moment in the history of the nation. Students become lost in a swamp of factual information, and as a consequence lose track of how those facts fit together, and why they are significant and relevant to the world today.

In this series, our effort has been to strip the vast amount of available detail down to a central core. Our aim is to draw in bold strokes, providing enough information, but no more than is necessary, to bring out the basic themes of the American story, and what they mean to us now. We believe that it is surely more important for students to grasp the underlying concepts and ideas that emerge from the movement of history, than to memorize an array of facts and figures.

The difference between this series and many standard texts lies in what has been left out. We are convinced that students will better remember the important themes if they are not buried under a heap of names, dates, and places.

In this sense, our primary goal is what might be called citizenship education. We think it is critically important for America as a nation and Americans as individuals to understand the origins and workings of the public institutions which are central to American society. We have asked ourselves again and again what is most important for citizens of our democracy to know so they can most effectively make the system work for them and the nation. For this reason, we have focused on political and institutional history, leaving social and cultural history less well developed.

This series is divided into volumes that move chronologically through the American story. Each is built around a single topic, such as the pilgrims, the Constitutional Convention, or immigration. Each volume has been written so that it can stand alone, for students who wish to research a given topic. As a consequence, in many cases material from previous volumes is repeated, usually in abbreviated form, to set the topic in its historical context. That is to say, students of the Constitutional Convention must be given some idea of relations with England, and why the revolution was fought, even though the material was covered in detail in a previous volume. Readers should find that each volume tells an entire story that can be read with or without reference to other volumes.

Despite our belief that it is of the first importance to outline sharply basic concepts and generalizations, we have not neglected the great dramas of American history. The stories that will hold the attention of students are here, and we believe they will help the concepts they illustrate to stick in their minds. We think, for example, that knowing of Abraham Baldwin's brave and dramatic decision to vote with the small states at the Constitutional Convention will bring alive the Connecticut Compromise, out of which grew the American Senate.

Each of these volumes has been read by esteemed specialists in its particular topic; we have benefited from their comments.

CHAPTER I

England on the Eve of Colonization

The role of Virginia in the creation of the United States was enormous. It was the first English colony to be permanently established on the mainland. Its people were usually in the forefront of the battle for the rights of Americans against the English government. A Virginian, Thomas Jefferson, wrote the Declaration of Independence. Another Virginian, George Washington, led the ragtag American army to its astonishing victory over the supposedly unbeatable British. Washington also presided over the Constitutional Convention of 1787 which produced the great document, so much admired worldwide, by which we still live. Yet another Virginian, James Madison, contributed many of the ideas which found their way into the Constitution. One more Virginian, George Mason, wrote the model on which our Bill of Rights is based. Four of the first five presidents were Virginians. Through wealth, talent, and the cultivation of the intellect, Virginia was, for the first two centuries of its history, the most influential colony in English America. Without Virginia, the history of the United States would have been substantially different.

In particular, there occurred in Virginia in its earliest years two developments that would profoundly affect America right down to the present moment. One was the establishment of the first legislative body in North America, the first attempt by American settlers to gain control of their own affairs and diminish interference from England. The second was the introduction of slavery, which over time came to be a powerful psychological force in America. These institutions, slavery and representative government, form an unhappy paradox, for one of them speaks to freedom and the other to its very opposite. How these two opposing institutions could rise together in the same place at exactly the same moment is one of the essential stories of American history.

Virginia had not been, at first, a focus for European colonization. Indeed, the first Europeans to visit what came to be called the New World were not primarily interested in starting colonies at all. Their concern was finding wealth. The first Europeans to reach America were probably some Irishmen, who in the 800s landed on Iceland, and may have gone on to land on the North American continent. They were followed later by Norse explorers who established little settlements in Greenland and Newfoundland. But there was not much to gain in such places, and these first explorations came to nothing and passed into legend. (For more detail on the early explorations of America, see *Clash of Cultures*, the first book of this series.)

Then, in 1492, Christopher Columbus made his famous voyage to the Caribbean. His aim was not colonization, or even to find new lands, but to reach what Europeans called "The Indies"—India, China, Japan, and the rest of Asia—in order to trade for silks, spices and other goods of immense value in Europe. Columbus made later voyages, and other Europeans followed him. The Spanish and Portuguese very rapidly overran much of Mexico, and Central and South America, bringing disease, slavery and death to the native Americans, and making off with vast shiploads of gold, silver and precious jewels.

Occupied as they were with the southern half of the New World, the

In most parts of the world, most people were tied to the land and had to obey the rules of their masters, the lords who owned the great estates where the people worked. In this picture from the 1300s, we see people engaged in the tasks that made up their lives as the seasons went around: plowing the fields; sowing the seeds; harrowing the fields; reaping the crops and carrying them home to the barns.

Spanish and Portuguese paid much less attention to the northern half. It was natural territory for the English, who were relatively closer to it, to exploit. They were, nonetheless, for reasons we shall look at shortly, slow to get going, in considerable part because English kings of the time, Henry VII and his son Henry VIII, had problems at home to worry about. But as they watched the Spanish in particular grow rich and powerful from the wealth they were carting out of the New World, the English grew fearful and jealous.

Then, in 1558, Elizabeth I became queen of England. She took over a nation divided by a number of religious and political issues. An intelligent and politically astute woman, much admired by the English people, she was able, at least temporarily, to smooth over the factional quarrels, which most English people were heartily tired of anyway. Throughout her reign, which lasted until 1603, England enjoyed a great flowering of the arts and sciences, with the emergence of great writers such as William Shakespeare and Edmund Spenser and composers such as William Byrd and John Dowland. A wave of confidence swept over the nation; the English people began to feel that they were to be a grand and glorious nation. And when, in

Life for the peoples of Europe revolved around villages like the one centered on the church seen in the background. It was rare for agricultural people to travel as much as ten miles from their homes. This picture from a Flemish calendar was made in the early 1500s, when people's eyes were first turning toward the New World.

1588, the English fleet, helped by a lucky storm, defeated the Spanish Armada of ships that had come to destroy them, they were sure they were a people of destiny. They must not let the Spanish get the upper hand. There were also a good many less romantic, more pragmatic and material reasons why the English began looking westward, which we shall look at shortly.

The fact that it was the English, not the Spanish or another European nation, who settled North America was of the most critical importance to the way what became the United States developed over the past four hundred years. With so many Americans today new immigrants, or the children and grandchildren of immigrants, it is easy to lose sight of the fact that for the first two hundred years of our history most of the inhabitants were English born, or of English descent. Inevitably, our institutions, however much they have changed over time, grew out of English ones. Without question, the first model for America was England.

The English were not alone in settling North America. The Dutch quite early built colonies along the Hudson River; the French settled large portions of what is now Canada; the Spanish established themselves in a small way in Florida and the Southwest; and both the Swiss and Swedish erected tiny colonies on the Delaware River. The cultural impact of these groups, especially the Dutch in New York and later the Germans in Pennsylvania, was significant.

But the vast majority of the settlers were English, and over time English culture became wholly dominant. Our language is English. Our system of law was adapted from the English one. Protestant Christianity, the religion of most Americans until the mid 1800s, was the English version. The literature we study in our schools and colleges including such masterpieces as *The Merchant of Venice*, *To a Skylark*, or *A Christmas Carol*, were written by English men and women. Indeed, so were some of our most enduring children's classics such as *Alice in Wonderland*, *Peter Rabbit*, *The Wind in the Willows*, and *Winnie-the-Pooh*. Many of our nursery rhymes are English: children today still hear about Banbury Cross, crooked sixpence, and Lord Mayors of London. Our great university system was built on English models: our first college, Harvard, founded only six years after the establishment of Massachusetts, was planned by men from Emmanuel College of Cambridge University in England.

We must always bear in mind, of course, that immigrants from places other than England have profoundly affected American government, American literature, American language, American sports. The influence of blacks and Jews in sports, entertainment and literature, for instance, and the Irish, Italians, Hispanics and many others in shaping our big cities, has been substantial. But however much American institutions have evolved, they were rooted in English systems, and still hold much of their original shape.

Just as important, we Americans have preserved some very basic attitudes brought here initially by English men and women. "Attitudes" are hard to pin down, but some are clear. In particular, English people of the time of the first settlements along the Atlantic Coast had a sense of personal liberty that was probably stronger than that of most other peoples. In most places all across the world the great majority of people were farm laborers "tied" to the land as peons, serfs, peasants—the term varied from place to place. They had no choice but to spend their lives working on land belonging to others, like great lords with huge estates passed down from generation to generation. They were given little or no education, and earned only just enough to keep themselves and their families in plain food and shelter. They had very few rights, but could be ordered about, within a few limits, by their masters—the local lord, the bishop, a royal official.

The situation in England was a little different. Beginning back at least as early as 1215, with the famous Magna Carta, Englishmen had begun developing the idea that there ought to be limits to what their rulers could order them to do. A small step at a time, the powers of the mighty were curtailed. By the early 1600s, English people expected that they could not be imprisoned on a whim and that government officials could not search their homes just because they wanted to. They felt they should be guaranteed fair trials by juries when they got into trouble. They had also established the principle of representative government, which permitted some of them to elect their own legislators.

To be sure, only a minority had the right to vote; and it was also true that powerful people often got around plain people's rights. Nonetheless, by the time of the first English settlements in America, English people quite firmly believed that they had certain rights which kings, lords, and the rich ought not to interfere with. This attitude toward personal liberty has become a central and deeply ingrained element of American attitudes.

Over the centuries, Englishmen had gained certain traditional rights that were not generally available to people in other European countries. One of the earliest steps toward modern American democracy was the issuing of Magna Carta in 1215, which to some extent curtailed the powers of the English king.

The significance to Americans of the development of these traditional rights in England was recognized by an exhibition of a rare copy of Magna Carta at Jamestown in 1957. Here Elizabeth II and her husband, Prince Philip, examine the great document.

Because so much of the way Americans think and go about things comes from seventeenth-century England, we need to see who these English people were. To begin with, while English people may have grumbled about taking orders from the wealthy and powerful above them, most of them accepted the idea that society was a ladder, with everybody assigned a certain rung. It seemed to most people that the class system was ordained by God, something so natural to human life that things simply could not be any other way. Undoubtedly the people higher up on that ladder believed in the inevitability of the system a good deal more firmly than those lower down. There was an old English saying that ran:

> *When Adam delved [dug] and Eve span [spun]*
> *Who was then a gentleman?*

suggesting that at least some people questioned God's establishment of the class system. Nonetheless, while ordinary people may have chafed under the rule of those higher up, they accepted it.

It is important that we understand this widespread acceptance of the right of the rich and powerful to rule, for one of the great movements that was to develop in Virginia was the attempt of people, through elected representatives, to gain power for themselves.

In England, the king and a small group of powerful noblemen whose support the king needed were at the top of the class system. Below them were the lesser nobles, and a larger group of people called "gentlemen," who usually owned large estates, with manor houses, barns, fields and woods and peasants to work the lands. Further down were yeomen, independent farmers who owned, or had rights to, some land and a farmhouse. And in the seventeenth century men engaged in commerce were beginning to form a new and influential class.

This upper layer of English society amounted to about ten percent of the population. They were, in effect, by position, birth and custom, the government, and acted not just in the king's court and in Parliament, but as judges, mayors, town officials.

Some of the ordinary people had their own little cottages with thatched roofs, and a barn and a garden. But perhaps half of English people were landless, poor, and at the mercy of those who held the land. These people lived hard lives, hiring out their labor to farmers, often sleeping in barns and eating the poorest kind of food. Among this great mass of English poor were tens of thousands of outright rogues, who lived by thievery, cheating, and gambling, sometimes in little bands sleeping in hovels in forests, much as had their famous predecessor, Robin Hood. This great mass of marginal English people snatched what pleasure they could from liquor, gambling, and dancing, but most of their lives were spent at back-breaking labor—cutting, wood, reaping wheat, digging ditches from first light until nightfall, with nothing to look forward to but a rough supper and a heap of straw for a bed.

You will notice that women are very rarely mentioned in this class system. That is because, strictly speaking, they did not belong to it. A woman's social role was determined by her husband's place on the ladder.

Women had far fewer rights than men. Their husbands were their masters in most respects. In this detail from a sixteenth-century painting by the great artist Peter Breugel, we see women setting off for the fields for their day's work

THE COVNTER SCVFFLE.
VVhereunto is added,
THE COVNTER RAT.

Written by R, S.

LONDON,
Printed by *Richard Bishop.* 1637.

Drunken rioting was so commonplace in England in the 1600s that it was the subject of humorous pictures and stories.

Women could not own property—it belonged to their husbands or fathers—although by the 1600s that was beginning to change. Women could not vote—most men could not vote, either—and they certainly could not aspire to become judges, professors, or lawyers, even though there had recently been a woman on the throne of England for almost half a century. However much influence women might have with their husbands, they were nonetheless clearly subordinate to men, not just in England, but in most places in the world.

Relatively few people lived outside of this land-based system. Among them were the clergy—ministers, preachers, church officials—who were supported by their parishioners or the local gentry. There were sailors and fishermen, and a fair number of artisans, like coopers who made barrels, smiths who forged nails and horseshoes, and weavers who made cloth. Such artisans passed their skills on down to their sons and nephews— indeed, in many places it was illegal for a man to take up a trade he had not inherited. Some of these artisans moved into the rising class of merchants who were beginning to challenge the landed aristocracy for political influence. But the bulk of the people were tied to the land and most of them were poor.

This way of life had existed in England, indeed much of Europe, for centuries. But now, in the years leading up to 1600, things were changing. And in those changes lay much of the impulse that swept England in the 1600s to emigrate to North America.

CHAPTER II

Capitalism and Colonialism

The three-thousand-mile trip across the Atlantic on tiny sailing ships took several weeks, or even months, depending on wind and weather. Those small ships rocked and pitched constantly. Illness aboard was routine, and if the trip took too long there would be shortages of food and water (or beer, which was thought to be safer to drink than water). Once in the new land, the immigrants were subject to Indian attack, to food shortages that frequently led to outright starvation, and to serious illness: the great *majority* of the first comers to North America died within a few years, or even a few months, of their arrival. Why on earth would anyone want to give up the comforts of a settled land to face pain, hunger, disease, and death in this strange country, filled with even stranger people?

There were several things happening to English society that drove English people to make the desperate trip. One of the most important was massive unemployment. The population of England had increased from about three million in 1500 to perhaps five million in 1650. There simply was not work enough for all these people. Making matters worse, many big landholders were switching from growing wheat and other grain to

One of the most famous episodes in the religious wars of the 1600s was the Gunpowder Plot of 1605, involving Guy Fawkes, a Roman Catholic. Fawkes and his fellow conspirators, determined to get more rights for their religion, attempted to blow up Parliament. They were caught before they could light the gunpowder they had smuggled into the basement of the Parliament building. A drawing made at the time shows the conspirators.

raising sheep, which took much less labor. In the process a lot of people lost their farm jobs, and wandered the countryside picking up what work they could, begging and stealing when they couldn't find any. By 1600, this large mass of unemployed were causing problems. Drunken rioting in the streets was commonplace. Thievery, mischief, cursing, and fighting were daily occurrences in village streets and town squares. It seemed to many people that things had not always been that way.

A second problem was the growing conflict between Parliament and the English monarchs. Parliament was different from a modern legislature, and was chosen by the rich and powerful, about five percent of the people. Under Queen Elizabeth, who was much loved and who understood compromise, things ran relatively smoothly. But her successors, the Stuart kings, were autocratic, and believed that their word should be law. Throughout the early 1600s, king and Parliament were locked in a desperate struggle, which would eventually break into civil war. This internal conflict was a source of worry and confusion for English people.

A print showing the execution of the Gunpowder Plotters. The print was made in Holland and is somewhat fanciful.

Yet another issue splitting England was religion. Henry VIII had eliminated Roman Catholicism, and made himself head of what now was the Anglican (that is, English) church. Nonetheless, many English people wanted to stick with Roman Catholicism. At the same time there was rising a strong movement "protesting" against what they saw as too much wealth and ceremony in both Roman and Anglican churches at the expense of true religious feeling. These Protestants wished to "purify" the church; and ultimately, of course, many of these Puritans immigrated to the wilderness of New England to worship as they liked. Religion, thus, was dividing England into several factions.

Actually, the religious and political wars overlapped. The king was head of the church, and naturally sided with the Anglicans against the Puritans, while many members of Parliament tended to be on the Puritan side. Unfortunately, emotions were strong, and as one side or another gained power, people were jailed, or even burned at the stake for their religious opinions.

Finally, there was going on at the same time a profound, slow-growing and subtle shift in the English economy. For centuries, land was wealth and wealth was land. Now there was a gradual switch to a "money economy," based on trade—the system we today call *capitalism*. The basic idea of the new system was that if a man had some capital, that is, a stock of money, however small, he could invest it in something with the hope of making a profit. He might buy a supply of wool, have it spun into yarn and woven into cloth, which he could sell for a good price. There were many ways enterprising men could multiply their money. Indeed, it was possible to become an entrepreneur without money, if you had a good idea and could persuade some wealthy man to finance you.

Capitalism led to yet another new system, the "stock company," in which several, even a great many, people would invest together in a large enterprise. These stock companies were the basis of the modern corporations that dominate the American and international economies today.

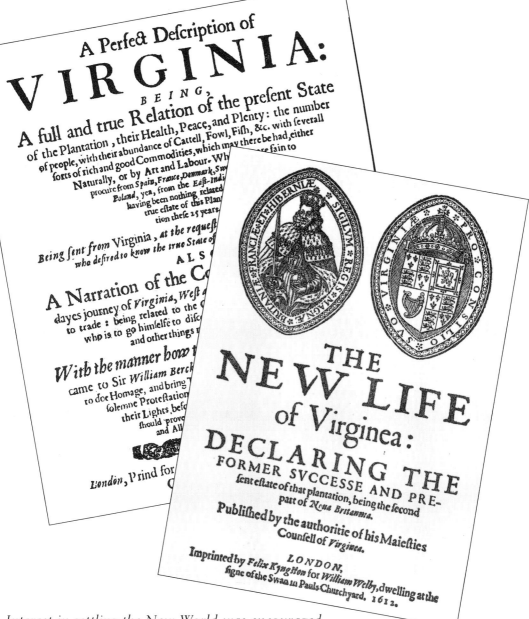

Interest in settling the New World was encouraged by many pamphlets, books, and broadsides. Here are two of the many examples of publications issued to advertise the Virginia plantation.

They proved important to the settlement of America, for many of the early colonies were supported by investors gathered in stock companies.

The switch from a land-based system of wealth to the money economy of capitalism took centuries to complete, but it changed the nature of life for the people involved. A lot of big landowners slowly lost power to businessmen building up their wealth through trade or manufacturing. For ordinary people, it meant a shift from the ancient life on the farm to jobs in factories and offices in towns and cities.

All of these things—massive unemployment, the religious and political battling, the new capitalism—made many thoughtful English people believe the nation was in trouble. They began to turn their eyes westward. It seemed obvious that the colonies could be filled with the unruly unemployed. In turn, many of those same unemployed felt they might be better off taking a chance on the wilderness, rather than facing the risk of starvation and jail at home. Many small farmers, and even a good many gentlemen, especially second sons who would not inherit any land, felt it was worth gambling on the new land. Religious dissenters, like the famous Mayflower Pilgrims, saw America as a last hope.

Most critically, the new capitalists believed that there was money to be made in North America, in timber, fish, furs, and other items. Throughout the early 1600s, interest in North America rose. It was fueled by writers exploiting this interest, who issued tracts and pamphlets on the new land. Much of this material was fanciful and inaccurate, but that only added to the interest. Among the best of them was Richard Haklyut, whose writing on America was reasonably accurate. He urged the settlement of North America by the English before other nations took it over. And so the movement to build an extension of England in the New World began—the first step on the road to the modern United States.

CHAPTER III

Indians Greet
the Englishmen

The English, in fact, had not been ignoring America entirely. There had been Bristol fishermen working the North Atlantic perhaps before Columbus's voyages, and throughout the 1500s the English, along with people of other nations, fished off the coast of North America. Other English explorers went out looking for the fabled water "passage" through America to the Indies. Still others went out as little more than pirates, to attack the Spanish treasure ships sailing from the Caribbean heaped with gold, silver and jewels. Some sailors managed to find their way around the tip of South America to the Far East and in many cases did bring back very profitable cargoes, mainly of spices.

But these were individual efforts, not part of any grand plan. Queen Elizabeth was a prudent, even cautious woman, not given to splashy adventures, as many English kings were. But it was clear that if England were to be great, it could not allow other nations, especially France, Holland, Spain or Portugal, who were building empires, to occupy all of the new land. Elizabeth had around her many bold men who were eager to colonize America, and in 1578, she granted one of them, Humphrey Gilbert, the right to occupy whatever land he could get hold of. Gilbert took several years to get organized, but in 1583 he sailed with five small ships and a party of colonists that included skilled craftsmen of various sorts who could build houses and mine for metals. The trip was a disaster. The little fleet reached what is now called Newfoundland, and headed south. Along the way two of the ships sank. Gilbert was in one of them and drowned along with hundreds of others.

Gilbert's fate might have discouraged many men, but it did not discourage one of Elizabeth's favorite courtiers, Walter Raleigh. He had already achieved much for himself. He was born a gentleman in a relatively poor family, but he grew to be tall, handsome, bold, intelligent—something of a daredevil, in fact. He wangled his way into court, where he caught the eye of Queen Elizabeth. He very quickly became one of her favorites, to the point where he hoped he might one day marry her.

Sir Walter Raleigh, a favorite of Elizabeth I, persuaded his queen to sponsor explorations of North America. His efforts to settle Virginia failed, but they encouraged others to try again.

Raleigh was Humphrey Gilbert's half brother. He also knew Richard Haklyut. Inevitably, he became enthusiastic about America. He persuaded the Queen to let him send out a party to search out likely spots for colonization. The Queen was too fond of him to let him go himself, but in 1584, he sent out a small fleet of ships, which returned with a bag of pearls, two Indians, and glowing reports about America, especially the area around Roanoke Island. The human beings who first peopled what we now call the Americas have traditionally been called Indians, because the first Europeans who landed in the Americas thought they had reached India. The term *Indians* is therefore not very accurate, and other terms have been used: *Amerinds*, and more recently, *Native Americans*. The Indians had no term for themselves, as they thought they were all the human beings that there were. Today most of them refer to themselves as Indian, and we will use that term here, while understanding that it is not very accurate. The Indians living there were "most gentle, loving, and faithful, void of all guile. . . ." The land was full of game, the report said, and the soil so rich crops grew without any assistance from man.

These reports were exaggerated, perhaps unknowingly, but they were all Raleigh and his supporters needed. Raleigh now brought young Richard Haklyut in to talk to Elizabeth. Haklyut made the point that, because of the riches flowing in from America, Spain was poised to dominate all of Europe. It was essential for England to curtail, and if possible destroy, the Spanish colonies in the New World. The English might get some help from the thousands of Indians the Spanish had enslaved, along with blacks brought in from Africa. A few of these people had already revolted against their Spanish masters; with the help of English soldiers and guns, the slaves might well overthrow the Spanish, whom they vastly outnumbered.

This line of argument persuaded Elizabeth. She authorized Raleigh to start a colony in what he decided to call Virginia, in honor of the virgin queen. In addition, at the same time that Raleigh's group went out, a ruthless adventurer, Sir Francis Drake, was to set out for the Caribbean with a small fleet of ships, to destroy Spanish colonies, take plunder, and free the black and Indian slaves to rise up against the Spanish.

It was an exceedingly daring plan, but it failed to take into account one important fact: the New World was already occupied by millions of Indians. The attitude of the Europeans was based partly on ignorance, and partly on arrogance. They had no awareness of the richness of the native American culture, but believed Indians to be grunting savages scraping hard livings from the wilderness. They also believed that the Indians were not using most of the land, unaware that what seemed to them empty forest was in fact the Indians' hunting grounds. They further believed that European culture was so superior to the Indian culture

Sir Francis Drake was a courageous and very tough seaman who plundered Spanish treasure ships that were taking jewels and gold back from their conquests around the Caribbean, but he did little to colonize the new lands.

that they would be doing the Indians a favor to bring them the blessings of civilization and Christianity. As it happened, the Indians were not much interested in either.

The Indians of North America were a varied group, speaking many different languages, living diverse lives, and getting their livings in many different ways. (Readers interested in the Indian way of life can find it in *Clash of Cultures*, the first book of this series.) The Indians with whom the Jamestown colonists had to contend were part of the Algonquian group, who occupied the eastern seaboard from Georgia on up into Maine. They spoke several languages, and their ways of life varied somewhat, but in general they followed the same pattern throughout the area.

They lived in small villages of at most a few hundred people. Their dwellings were framed out of saplings dug into the ground and covered with hides, sheets of bark, or mats woven of reeds. These dwellings could be easily pulled apart and moved to another location, when the soil wore out after several years.

Corn was their main staple, but they also grew pumpkins, squash, and various types of beans, usually planting them among the corn, so that the bean vines could climb the cornstalks. The gardens were worked by the women, with the help of the children. The women also ground the corn into meal, and prepared the food.

The men hunted and fished, made boats by hollowing out big logs, and did the other heavy work needed. In the fall, there was always a deer hunt. The women would skin the deer after the hunt, dry the meat for storage through the winter, and prepare the deer skins to be made into clothing.

Life was surprisingly easy for most Indian tribes. The Chesapeake Bay area around Jamestown was particularly rich in resources: deer, squirrels, and rabbits in the forests; oysters and clams in the bay; a variety of fish in the rivers; wild berries, fruits, and nuts growing in the woods and fields. The Indians customarily did not produce any more food than they needed. They grew only enough corn to last them through the winter, and sometimes not even that, so that there was often a hungry period in the early spring, a fact that would be of considerable importance to the English settlers. Nor did they believe in owning anything more than what they really needed. Anything extra was just that much more to carry when they moved to new ground. This attitude was quite different from that of the English settlers, who wanted to pile up things and grow rich.

Because they worked only as much as they had to, the Indians had a good deal of spare time, which they used for having fun—dancing, playing sports and games, telling stories and legends. To the English, the Indians appeared lazy; but in the Indians' opinion, it made no sense to do more work than was necessary for a comfortable way of life.

Further, the Indians did not have the same ideas about land ownership that the English had. As they saw it, the land was almost a person, and like any person, belonged to itself. It could be *used* by human beings, but not *owned* as Europeans owned land. The Indians saw the land somewhat as the English saw air: something not generally owned, but used by everybody.

A major preoccupation of Indian males was war. All boys were trained from childhood in the use of the bow, the war club, and how to take scalps. Prisoners of war were frequently tortured to death in painful ways. Sometimes all their joints would be cracked one at a time. Sometimes they would be slowly burned, first one foot, then the next, then a hand. Torturing a warrior so he could show bravery was considered an honor to him, and young Indian boys were taught songs to sing while they were being tortured to death, so they could show their scorn for the pain they were suffering.

Surprisingly, Indian wars were less bloody than European ones. In a certain sense, the Indians thought of war as a kind of deadly sport. Indian males felt they had to go to war frequently to show their courage and hardiness, or to get revenge on an enemy tribe, but the fighting was usually

One thing that both attracted and threatened the Indians was superior European technology. The Indians were extremely skilled at fashioning stone tools, such as this ax head, but they traded for English metal hatchets whenever they could.

short and swift. Often one band would raid an enemy village in a surprise attack at dawn, take a few scalps, capture a few prisoners, possibly steal some corn or burn some houses, and then leave. There would be a minimum of people killed. As a rule, when an Indian group saw that it was outmanned, it would retreat and later pay tribute in the form of some furs, skins, or corn, to indicate its acceptance of the other group's superiority. This was yet one more way in which Indians and English ideas differed, and when it came to fighting it put the Indians at a disadvantage.

But there was one critical fact that neither the Indians nor the Europeans knew at first, although both discovered it soon enough. For reasons we do not thoroughly understand, many diseases common in Europe had never reached the New World, among them smallpox, measles, and the plague. These diseases, even measles, were scourges, killing thousands of Europeans each year. Nonetheless, over time Europeans had acquired a measure of natural immunity; the majority of adults who caught smallpox recovered from it, although they might be permanently scarred.

The Indians did not have a natural immunity to these diseases, and as contact with whites grew in the decades after Columbus's arrival, the diseases swept through the people of America as terrible epidemics. Not merely whole villages, but whole clusters of villages were wiped out, leaving only a few survivors. Thus, while the land the English were coming to was not unoccupied, it is true that is was to an extent underpopulated.

It was the plan of Elizabeth and her favorites, Raleigh and Drake, to treat the Indians with kindness. After the evil treatment the Indians had received from the Spanish, the English believed that they would be happy to have English overlords, accept Christianity, and cover their nakedness with English clothes, not incidentally providing a splendid market for English wool. In thinking thus the English were not so much being arrogant as naïve. Most people, without giving it much thought, believe their own ways are best. The English did; but so did the Indians, and they were no more interested in adopting Christianity and English dress than the English were in worshiping Indian gods and wearing loincloths and feathered headdresses.

It was with high hopes that, in 1585, Raleigh and Drake set out on their missions. Drake's expedition was, on the whole, successful. He missed a large Spanish treasure fleet on its way home from the Caribbean, but he destroyed a number of Spanish outposts in the Caribbean area, taking a lot of plunder and freeing thousands of Indian and African slaves.

Meanwhile, Raleigh sent off his little fleet under the command of Sir Richard Grenville. Included in the company were three hundred sailors to man the ships, a couple of hundred soldiers, and 108 men designated as "colonists." At that time, most of the men in the English army and navy were conscripts, many of whom had been "impressed" into the service against their will. Typically, these people were taken from the unemployed laborers wandering the English countryside in search of work.

To attempt to build a colony with such people was a mistake. Few of them had any real interest in the success of the venture; most of them wanted only to be back home, and as a result few of them had much desire to do the hard work establishing a colony requires. Making matters worse, Grenville's two commanders were both hot-tempered soldiers who were more interested in fighting than in building a peaceable colony.

However, going along on the trip was a painter named John White, who, to our great good luck, made a series of excellent paintings of Indians and the landscape which have been very helpful to historians in understanding the America of the time.

The expedition reached the Carolinas in June, 1585, and Grenville set himself up in business on Roanoke Island, which lay inside the barrier islands not far from where Kitty Hawk is today. Unfortunately, the ship carrying much of the supplies for the colonies went aground, and the supplies were ruined. It was an omen.

A more important omen was the now famous incident of the silver cup. During an exploration of the mainland, an Indian stole a valuable silver cup. Grenville sent a party of soldiers to an Indian village where they suspected it was hidden. When the Indians could not, or would not, produce the cup, the English burned the village in revenge, drove out the people, and trampled down their cornfields. It was a stupid thing to do, for it got relations between the English and the Indians off to a very bad start.

A worse problem was the failure of the English to start planting corn, and otherwise prepare themselves to be self-sufficient. Instead, they demanded corn from the Indians, who gave it, but reluctantly. The Indians usually planted only enough corn to get through the winter, and they had little to spare. The basic problem was that, whatever idea they had of showing kindness to the Indians, the English leaders were warriors who were used to pushing other people around; and the sailors, soldiers, and "colonists" were an unruly bunch who refused to do any ordinary work.

Grenville returned home in August, leaving the colony to struggle along, getting food any way it could, which mainly meant bullying the Indians for it. There were battles, and finally the English took the

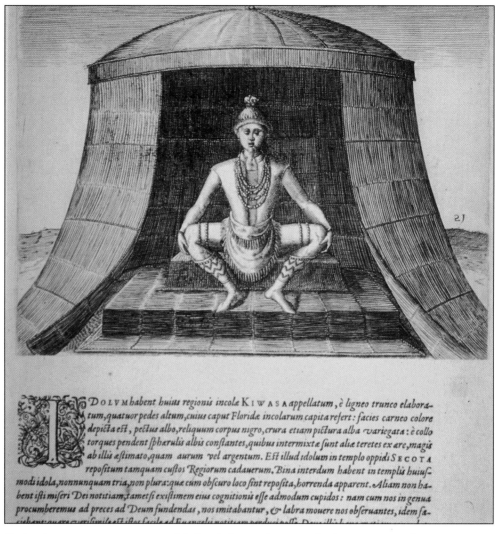

Raleigh sent a painter named John White, along with the scientist Thomas
Hariot, on an early trip to Virginia. On their return, Hariot wrote a description
of the new land. Since there was no way to reproduce colored pictures in a book,
an engraver named Theodor de Bry was hired to copy the pictures in black-and-
white engravings. The Hariot book was widely distributed, and the de Bry pictures had a great influence on Europeans' ideas of the Indians. This engraving
shows the Indian idol Kiwasa, carved of wood and set in a small temple.

The de Bry pictures were republished many times, often in slightly different versions. Here we see an Indian "conjurer," or medicine man. According to Hariot, conjurers often talked to devils. The original de Bry picture, copied from John White's watercolor, is at left. At right, a later version, which was hand colored.

Roanoke Indian chief by surprise and killed him and some others. Once again it was a foolish thing to do, for the English were badly outnumbered and short of almost everything they needed to survive. In the end they gave up, and when Drake appeared with his fleet, they boarded his ships and sailed for home.

Unbeknownst to them, supply ships were already on the way from England, again under the command of Grenville. He reached Roanoke to find the place deserted. Leaving a handful of soldiers to hold the ground, he left for the Caribbean to plunder the Spanish, which must have seemed

There are several historic parks that have reconstructed old towns and villages according to careful historic study. These parks often offer reenactments of events and daily life as it was then. This reenactment shows an Indian making cordage, that is, rope. Behind him is a typical Indian dwelling of the eastern American seaboard. It is made of a framework of saplings covered with woven mats. In some cases, animal hides or sheets of bark were used to cover the framework.

Indians cooked their food over open fires. Much of it was broiled or grilled on sticks, but they also boiled meat, fish, and vegetables in pots set on stones over the fire.

Clay pots were used by Indians for storage, for carrying, and for cooking. Making them was a regular task for the women. In this reenactment, we see an Indian woman shaping a pot with a stick. Many pots were made with pointed bottoms so they could be stuck into the coals of a fire.

to him an easier way to get rich than planting colonies. The little group on Roanoke were left to their own resources, and when in July, 1587, the painter John White brought yet another group to Roanoke, among them his daughter and her husband, he also found the place deserted. The people Grenville had left had disappeared, presumably killed by the Indians.

White now began to understand that a colony in Virginia could not survive without ample provisions to get started with. He sailed for home to get supplies, but unluckily, before he could get things organized, the conflict with Spain heated up, giving the English government other things than colonization to worry about. But in 1588, the Spanish Armada sailed into a storm-blown English Channel and met disaster. Nevertheless, White did not get back to Roanoke until 1590. When he landed he discovered to his shock the place deserted, and his daughter and her husband gone, along with their child, who was the first English person known to have been born in America. All he found was the word "CROATAN" carved into a tree. Croatan was the name of a nearby Indian group, and it is thought that the colonists had run into problems, and had sought refuge with the Croatan Indians. However, there were also signs that the little colony may have been attacked. Romantics prefer to think that the colonists did indeed make it to the Croatan village, where over time they became absorbed into the tribe, and that the descendants of the Lost Colony are living among the present-day Croatans. But nobody knows for sure.

CHAPTER IV

Powhatan Loses a Daughter and the English Get Tobacco

The failure of Raleigh and his allies to establish a colony in the Virginia area, and particularly the tragic disappearance of the Lost Colony of Roanoke, discouraged English attempts to build a colony in North America—for the moment. Thoughtful people were disturbed by the great loss of life that had occurred among the colonists. Besides, the ventures had cost Raleigh, the Gilbert family, and even Queen Elizabeth, a great deal of money. The only rewards coming from overseas had been the plunder taken from the Spanish. It was time for a licking of wounds.

But there were still good reasons for colonizing the New World. Those tens of thousands of jobless English people continued to wander city streets and country lanes; and many people went on believing that a great deal of money could be made in America.

In 1603, Queen Elizabeth died. She was succeeded by James VI, King of Scotland, who now became also James I of England. James was autocratic, determined to run things as he wished. He needed money, and saw that if colonies were established, he could put taxes on the furs and other goods that were brought home from America. Better still, he would have his own source of raw materials essential for building ships for his navy, pinepitch and timber that he had been buying from the Baltic states. He granted a royal charter to a group of investors to establish a colony in Virginia. The charter, dated April 10, 1606, included permission to occupy much of the Atlantic coast of America.

Because it is important to the way constitutional democracy developed in America, we need to understand that a royal charter of this kind spelled out what sort of rights were granted to all the parties involved. In this case, James gave the stay-at-home "adventurers" who were "venturing" only their money in the colony the right to develop all the land from what is roughly now North Carolina up into Maine, running a hundred miles inland, a huge chunk of territory. Needless to say, neither James nor the adventurers consulted the Indians living there about it. A governing board in London, controlled by the king, would have final say-so on all matters. But it was clear that a board operating several weeks' sailing time away from the colony could hardly deal with day-to-day affairs, so there would be a thirteen-man council in Virginia, operating under English law, to manage the colony. The council would elect its own president. Clearly, the colonists would have, in practice, a certain measure of freedom from the English government at home.

The English had learned something from their earlier failures in colonizing America, but they had not learned enough. The colonists who set off in three ships early in 1607 were a mixture. Some of them had paid their own way. Some had signed on as indentured servants for seven years in exchange for their passage. Many of them were gentlemen, probably second sons who would not inherit much at home, and were looking for ways to build their own estates. These people had grown up with servants around, had never done much productive work, and apparently expected not to do any when they got to Virginia, either. Indentured servants, who were little short of slaves, had no reason to work any harder than they were forced to. Once again, the experiment was getting off on the wrong foot.

The planters—as they were called—knew, of course that the earlier Raleigh colonies had made enemies of the Indians around Roanoke. They therefore decided to settle further to the north. Haklyut had advised them to settle well up a river where they would have warning of approaching Spanish ships, and if possible, on a peninsula, which could be more easily defended. In addition, the river had to be deep enough for ocean-going ships.

When the little fleet reached Virginia, the colonists quickly found such a place on a river they named the James at a place they called Jamestown.

The Susan Constant, *a replica of one of the ships that carried settlers to Jamestown at the beginning. This replica can be seen today at Jamestown.*

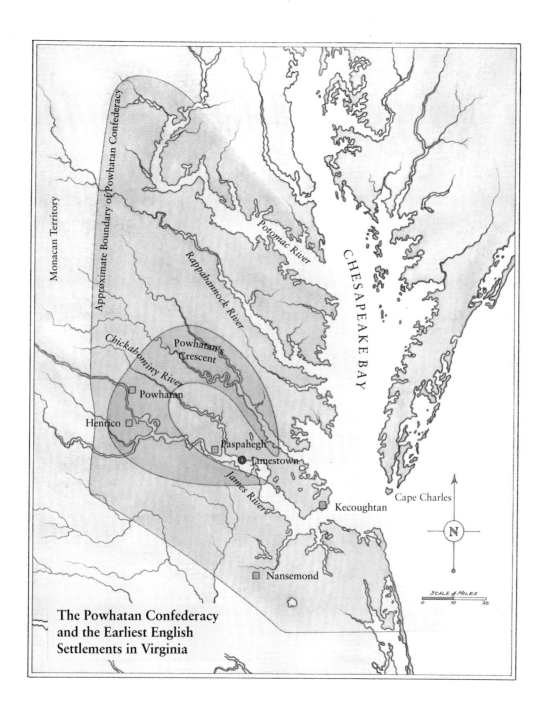

Monacan Territory

Approximate Boundary of Powhatan Confederacy

Potomac River

Rappahannock River

CHESAPEAKE BAY

Chickahominy River

Powhatan's
Crescent

Powharan

Henrico

Paspahegh

Jamestown

James River

Kecoughtan

Cape Charles

N

Nansemond

SCALE of MILES
0   10   20

**The Powhatan Confederacy
and the Earliest English
Settlements in Virginia**

The site had advantages, but it had disadvantages, too. For one, it was near swampy ground, a breeding place for diseases, especially deadly malaria. For another, it was right in the heart of a large Indian kingdom, ruled by a cunning and aggressive chief called Powhatan. The colony, clearly, had two strikes against it from the start.

In the years before the English settlers arrived in Virginia, Chief Powhatan had pulled all the Indians in the area between the York and James Rivers into a coalition of tribes amounting to some twelve thousand people. He did not have absolute control of all the groups in his domain. Some paid him regular tribute, but other, stronger groups kept him at arm's length. Nonetheless, he had a strong fighting force, and his authority in the area was considerable.

Powhatan was, in fact, no less arrogant than King James of England; indeed, he assumed he was equal, if not superior, to the English king. He would receive visitors lolling back on heaps of furs, surrounded by warriors and several wives. Clearly, Powhatan was not the sort of man who would allow a small group of strange people to wander around his domain as they liked. And when the very first men debarked from the English ships in April, 1607, they were attacked by Indians, who were driven off only by the shipboard cannons. Obviously, the English colony would survive only if Powhatan decided to tolerate them.

And for the moment he did. The English explored the area on May 14 and settled on the place near where Jamestown stands today. They set about building a fort and planting corn, and then a group led by the ship's captain made a trip upriver in a small boat, stopping at Indian villages along the way to explain that they had come in peace and wanted the Indians' friendship.

While they were gone, a group of Indians attacked the fort. Once again the settlers were saved only by the cannons from the ships.

The English had made a poor start, and from then on matters got worse. The settlers began to bicker among themselves. The ships weighed anchor and set off for home, taking with them the cannon that had twice saved the little settlement. And there were more fundamental problems. Although it should have been obvious that a great deal of hard work was needed to put the colony on its feet, a great many of the settlers refused to do very much. Gentlemen believed that they were above ordinary labor, and the indentured servants, knowing that profits from their work would go to others, declined to do any more than they could be forced to do.

Then disease struck. Food got short and people grew hungry. Hunger made the colonists more susceptible to disease than ever. They began to die in large numbers, and by September *half* the colonists were dead. The situation appeared to be hopeless.

In this crisis, a natural leader emerged from out of the pack. His name was John Smith. He had had, to say the least, an unusual life to this point. Born a yeoman, he had become a soldier and fought against the Turks, who were trying to press into Europe. He was captured in battle, and made a slave by the Turks. However, so he said, a beautiful Turkish princess was attracted to him, and helped him to escape. He made his way across Europe back to England.

Only twenty-seven in 1607, he was intelligent, brave and tough-minded. These were exactly the qualities the settlers needed, and it is to their credit that they let Smith take over. Smith quickly made a deal with the Indians for corn, which saved the colony for the moment.

Then befell one of the best-known tales of America's early days. That fall, Smith went out exploring the Chickahominy River. On the trip, he was captured by some of Powhatan's warriors, under the leadership of Opechancanough, whom modern historians believe to be Powhatan's brother. Smith spent a month with these Indians, learning their ways and scraps of their language. Finally he was taken to see the great Powhatan himself. He was in conversation with Powhatan, when suddenly some of the warriors who had formed a semi-circle around Smith, leapt on him, intent, he believed, on beating him to death with their clubs. Then,

King Powhatan *comands* C.Smith *to be* slayne *his daughter* Pokahontas *begs his life his* thankfullness *and how he* Subiected 39 *of their kings* reade *y* histor

An early woodcut showing the great chief Powhatan ordering that John Smith be slain, while Pocahontas begs for his life. The legend is probably not entirely correct, and this artist's version is certainly fanciful

according to Smith's recollection of the event, Powhatan's beautiful daughter flung herself against him, and saved his life. The princess was of course Pocahontas.

This is Smith's version of the story, of course. Generally speaking, Smith appears to have been a reasonably honest man, and these stories of beautiful princesses helping him to escape from trouble may have some truth to them. However, historians believe that he probably misinterpreted what was going on, and that what he took to be an attack was part of some kind of ceremony involving his admission to the tribe, or even marriage to Pocahontas.

In any case, the Indians released Smith. He returned to Jamestown to find only thirty-eight of the settlers alive. Finally, it appeared that hope for the colony was gone. But incredibly, on the very day that Smith rejoined the group, a ship from England came sailing up the river with more settlers and provisions. Yet it seemed as if the Jamestown colony's hard luck was endless: three days after the ship arrived a fire broke out in town, destroying most of it, along with the food that had come from England.

Powhatan, at this point, could easily have wiped out the colony; but for reasons we shall eventually see, he chose not to do so. When Smith appeared once more begging for help, Powhatan gave him corn, fish, and meat. Again the colony was saved—at least for the moment. A ship arrived from the West Indies with food, and in October, 1608, another ship came from England, bringing more provisions and seventy more settlers, including the first two women to reach Jamestown. Yet misfortune continued to rain down: rats from the ship ate most of the provisions. Again, Smith took charge. He organized fishing and hunting parties, and the colony staggered onward. That winter only a very few of the two hundred settlers died.

Meanwhile, Smith had written the story of the colony, which was published in England without his knowledge along with some surprisingly

Relations between the Indians and the Jamestown settlers were always uneasy and frequently bloody. Jamestown was in fact a fort, with armed soldiers always on guard. This is the fort entrance, as reconstructed according to careful study.

accurate maps he had made, showing the domains of the Indian tribes. Smith was now a star in England, and interest in the overseas colonies sharpened.

But relations with the Indians were going sour. In part this was Smith's fault. He had come to the conclusion that there was no use trying to get along with Indians. They were savages, as he saw it, and could not be trusted. They would have to be subjugated. More and more often he took raiding parties into Indian villages to plunder them for corn and other supplies. The Indians of course fought back and by the winter of 1609, there was open warfare between the two peoples. But Smith himself was soon gone. Some of the settlers, who would have been his social superi-

In the early days, all able-bodied men in the colony were required to undergo military training, and all had to fight when necessary. These men are drilling with spearlike pikes.

This drawing of Jamestown was made in 1622, when the little colony was finally struggling to its feet. It was surrounded by a wall in case of attack. At right we see smoke from a cannon firing at Indians in canoes.

ors back home, chafed under his orders and demanded his recall. Late in 1609, he was ordered back to London.

The English were now in a war they could not win. Powhatan besieged Jamestown and pinned the settlers in. The starving Englishmen ate their cattle and goats; when they were gone they ate the dogs, and then rats and mice. And when they were gone, the settlers started to eat each other. One man killed his wife, salted her and ate her. Others ate the bodies of those who had starved to death. Finally, in May, 1610, a ship arrived from the West Indies. The man in charge was so shocked by the condition of both the colonists and the town that he ordered Jamestown to be abandoned. The desperate adventure was finally over, or so it appeared. But then even as the colonists were on board ready to head back for England, there sailed up the James River three English ships with food, supplies, 150 new colonists and a hundred soldiers. Once again, the colony had been saved at the last hour.

Even so, it was far from certain that Jamestown could last. The colonists numbered only a few hundred. They were still not self-sufficient, growing less corn than they needed, and not skilled enough at hunting and fishing to feed themselves from the wilderness. Powhatan had several thousand healthy and well-armed warriors, who knew the country, and knew how to survive in the forest. He was clearly able to destroy the Jamestown colony if he wanted to. Why didn't he?

There were several reasons. For one thing, the Indians were to some extent awed by the English. English ships, English metal, and particularly English swords, knives and guns, were far superior to anything the Indians had. In truth, a trained Indian with a bow could shoot as accurately and much more rapidly than a soldier could with a musket. But there was something almost magical about guns, which with a flash, smoke, and a thunderous roar seemed to kill instantaneously. Even more important, the English possessed some magic that kept them safe from the diseases that killed Indians by the thousands. The English god, many Indians thought, was stronger than theirs.

But Powhatan was not a man easily awed. The main reason he did not wipe out the Jamestown colony was because he hoped he could use English soldiers and English weapons against his Indian enemies. Indian society, we recall, was webbed with rivalries between villages, tribes, and tribal groups like Powhatan's. Partnerships and coalitions formed and broke in ever-shifting patterns. There was always the danger of warfare breaking out somewhere. To Powhatan, the presence of the small Jamestown colony was nothing more than a stone in his shoe compared with the threat from large, ambitious tribes on his western frontier. He therefore was, in a sense, keeping the English in reserve as potential allies should he need them against attack from a rival. Although the English didn't at first realize it, divisions among the Indians would in the end allow the English to win. But Powhatan remained a formidable threat.

Yet the colony continued to stagger on from one crisis to the next. In 1611, new officials, Sir Thomas Dale and Deputy Governor Sir Thomas Gates, arrived. They were determined to make the colony work, in every sense of the word. They established something like military discipline. They forced everyone to plant corn, build houses, and do a lot of other work that should have been done much earlier. They also started other small settlements outside of Jamestown itself along the James River, with the idea and the hope that they would grow into towns. The stern discipline established by Dale and Gates improved things a good deal, but it was something else that would, in the end, allow Virginia to survive.

Tobacco had long been part of the Indian culture, smoked in pipes as part of ceremonies, or simply for pleasure. Columbus had brought tobacco back to Europe on his first voyage, and thereafter the habit of "drinking" the smoke of the plant began to spread through the Old World. By the time James I became King of England in 1603, the habit of smoking had become widespread. Clay pipes frequently hung on the walls of taverns so that customers could sit there and smoke.

James I disliked the habit of smoking tobacco, and even wrote a pamphlet against it. But he was powerless to stop it—as indeed has been the case with governments ever since. Most of the tobacco imported to Europe came from the Spanish West Indies, and sold in England at eighteen shillings a pound. This was an enormous price, almost a month's wages for an ordinary worker in England at the time. The Indians in the

Virginia area grew tobacco, and some of the settlers tried to grow some for export, too, but the tobacco was not up to the quality of the West Indian tobacco and did not sell.

Then a smart and enterprising colonist named John Rolfe got hold of some seeds of the West Indian tobacco. The tobacco he grew from them was still not as good as that grown in the Caribbean, but it was a lot better than the local Virginia variety. In 1614, Rolfe shipped some tobacco to England; it sold for three shillings a pound, not the price the Caribbean tobacco commanded, but still a very good price. When the other colonists saw the prices tobacco would bring, they rushed out to plant it, to the extent that the governor had to actually order people to spend some of their time planting corn so they would not starve.

In this story lies an important fact that the financial backers of the colony had not understood. From the beginning, keeping the colonists at the necessary hard work had been a constant problem. Even when they were without food many of them would spend their time idly bowling instead of exerting themselves to grow or find food. But now the colonists had before them a kind of work that would directly benefit themselves, and suddenly they were willing to work hard. From Rolfe's initial shipment of four barrels, tobacco output jumped to 2,300 pounds in 1616, and to 49,500 pounds two years later. At last, the colony had a way of making money, and for the first time there came a flicker of real hope that it might survive.

John Rolfe, however, is remembered for something other than introducing the tobacco trade to Virginia. The English managed to capture Pocahontas, and hold her for ransom. While she was in Jamestown she learned English manners and the Christian religion from two Englishmen. One of these was John Rolfe. He fell in love with her, and she with him. Governor Dale gave Rolfe permission to marry her; Powhatan also gave his permission. Pocahontas took the name Rebecca, and in April, 1614, they were married, with two of Powhatan's sons in attendance. For a

Matoaks als Rebecka daughter to the mighty Prince
Powhatan Emperour of Attanoughkomouck als Virginia
converted and baptized in the Christian faith and
Wife to the wor.ll Mr Tho: Rolff.

Pocahontas eventually married one of the colonists, John Rolfe. In 1616 she visited England, where a portrait of her wearing English clothing was painted.

By the end of the seventeenth century Virginia was growing rich on tobacco worked mainly by slaves. The leaves were dried in open sheds like this one before going off to market.

time, at least, peace between the English and Powhatan prevailed.

But peace was temporary. In 1617 and 1618, an epidemic of bubonic plague swept up the eastern seaboard from Florida into New England. Among those it killed was the great Chief Powhatan, who was by then old. His crown was inherited by Opechancanough, the man who had captured John Smith ten years earlier, and thus created the legend of Pocahontas. Opechancanough had many grievances against the English and he decided that he would once and for all drive them off the land. He

Caring for tobacco as it grew, harvesting it, and preparing it for shipment required a great deal of tedious hand labor. Workers were in short supply in Virginia, which is why the colonists eventually came to depend on slave laborers. Here a field hand is seen "topping" a tobacco plant.

bided his time and then in 1622, he struck, sending warriors into farms and villages up and down the James River to slaughter the English invaders and burn their farms. In one sweep, the Indians killed about a third of the settlers, 347 men, women and children.

If Opechancanough had followed up this initial onslaught with an attack on Jamestown itself, he almost certainly would have finished off the colony. But according to the Indian way of thinking, he assumed that the devastation of the first attack would discourage the English, and they would give up. Instead, it enraged them. They began to mount raids on the Indians, killing, burning villages, and taking corn. Finally, in July, 1624, a small body of sixty armed and armored Englishmen sailed into the heart of Powhatan territory, where they were met by some eight hundred Indian warriors. For once, the Indians stood and fought in open battle. They showed great courage and determination, but their arrows could not strike through English armor. For two days, the English banged away at the Indians, almost with impunity. A great many Indians were wounded and killed; only sixteen English were wounded, and none killed. The power of the Powhatan coalition was broken. Indians from other groups observed the battle, and took home the lesson that the English could not be beaten, no matter how badly outnumbered. There would be, for many years, occasional skirmishes between Indians and English, but the English had won. Virginia was to be theirs.

CHAPTER V

Representative Government Comes to Virginia

During the years from 1607, when the Virginia settlement was started, to the defeat of the Powhatan coalition in 1624, the colony had slipped and slid from one disaster to the next, pulled back from the edge of the cliff each time by chance as much as anything. All during these troubled years the stockholders in the Virginia Company back in London frantically kept trying one scheme after another to make the experiment a success. In the course of working up these improvised and hastily thought out programs, the Company officers continually tinkered with the system by which the battered colony was governed. What they ended up with was a government that had profound effects on the shape of the United States that was to come. We must now go back to the beginning to see how the Virginia government developed.

We need first to understand the differences between a *corporation*, with a joint stock charter, and a *royal colony*. The joint stock company was an association of private individuals. They were granted certain authority in their charter from the king, but they were nonetheless subject to the laws of the country, which for practical purposes in the case of Virginia meant the wishes of the king.

The Virginia Company was a joint stock company of this sort. It was run by a board at first appointed by the king, which would set the basic rules for the colony. Nonetheless, it was not an official part of the government. It was in this way similar to modern large corporations, like Ford or General Motors or AT&T: such corporations have a good deal of power, and can set rules for their employees, but they are not part of the government, and must obey laws coming out of Washington.

Obviously, the lines of authority between king, investors and colonists could be drawn in a lot of ways. The New England colonies that came along in the years after 1620 ended up having a good deal of control of their own affairs. On the other hand, colonies in Maryland and Pennsylvania that were started somewhat later were what was called "proprietary colonies"—that is, they were owned outright by a single person, for example William Penn in the case of Pennsylvania, who set the rules.

The government of the Virginia colony was somewhere between a charter colony run by its investors and a proprietary colony run by its owner. Originally it was to be run in England by a board appointed by the king, which would establish broad guidelines. But it took weeks, or even months, for messages to go back and forth across the Atlantic, and it was recognized from the outset that the colony needed the power to manage day-to-day affairs themselves. They would have a local council in Virginia, picked by the London board. This was by no means a democratic government—indeed democracy is hardly a word to use in connection with any English government of the seventeenth century. But the colonists were given rights they would have had in England, such as the right to trial by a jury.

But by 1609, the year that Jamestown was almost abandoned, it was clear that the colony needed firmer leadership. The colonists were forever bickering among themselves, and refusing to work even in the face of starvation. The London board asked the king to revise the charter. This

Making a success of these early colonies required a great deal of hard labor. Here a blacksmith is hammering a hot piece of iron into shape.

time there would be a Lord Governor, appointed by the London group. The Lord Governor would in turn appoint a council in Virginia which would have a good deal of power. This still was not a representative form of government, for power ran from the king, through the Virginian Company in London, to the Virginia Lord Governor and the council he had appointed.

Problems remained. Despite the semi-military government put in by Sir Thomas Dale and Sir Thomas Gates in 1611, the Jamestown colony still staggered from one crisis to the next. But with the sudden commercial success of tobacco, it became clear that the colonists would work if they individually had something to gain by it.

The Virginia Company in London was now dominated by a man

named Sir Edwin Sandys, (the y is silent) the son of the Archbishop of York, and thus a man of influence. Sandys was an intelligent and forthright man, one of those in Parliament trying to stand up against the autocratic King James. He was widely admired, and made himself the leader of a group among the Virginia Company's investors who were tired of waiting for their investment to pay off. In 1618, Sandys and his supporters decided to push through some reforms which might get the colony working more productively.

Early houses were made in the European fashion. A framework of beams was built, and the walls were filled in with a mixture of twigs, straw, mud, and clay. This man is daubing a wall with this mix.

Dishes and clothes had to be washed by hand with homemade soap in buckets. Here a woman does the dishes.

Sandys's group decided that the colonists might be more willing to obey the rules if they had a larger say in writing them. They therefore put in a new governor, Sir George Yeardly, who would as before choose a council to work with him. But—and this was a very big but—there would also be an assembly, called the House of Burgesses, that would be *elected* by the colonists. Each of the little Virginia settlements up and down the James River would choose two burgesses. Not everybody would vote. The original document has been lost, but what seems to be a copy of it says that the burgesses shall "bee espetially chosen by the inhabitants." The term "inhabitants" did not mean exactly what it means today. Historians think that, in fact, voting rights were limited to males who paid taxes or at least were not servants. Indeed, Governor Yeardly and his cohorts may have seen the House of Burgesses largely as an instrument of control through which they could dominate the course of events in Virginia.

Nevertheless, the creation of this elected legislative body, or assembly, was a fact of critical importance in American history. Hardly anywhere in the world did "the people" at large vote on anything, including government officials. Even in relatively advanced nations like Spain and France, power was held by a handful of rich aristocrats; ordinary people had little say in how they were ruled. England, which permitted a great deal more popular participation than most countries, allowed only well-to-do property owners to vote—probably no more than five percent of the population. Everybody else was powerless to affect what these people decided for them.

Wealthy Virginians could import furniture and other goods from England, and sometimes ordinary farmers imported such goods, too. Nonetheless, most things were handmade in the colony. Here a carpenter shapes a table leg from a branch.

In setting up the elected House of Burgesses, the Virginia company was by no means creating a democracy in the modern sense. The assembly would meet only once a year, except in emergency, and at one point no elections were held for fourteen years and the same burgesses met year after year. The governor could veto the laws that it passed, and in any case, eventually laws would have to be approved by the Virginia Company back in London. Nonetheless, in practice the House of Burgesses did have a good deal of real power. It could discuss anything it wanted, and initiate legislation, making its wishes known. Sensible governors knew that there was not much point in shoving laws down the throats of the Burgesses, for such laws would be hard to enforce.

The creation of the House of Burgesses in Virginia in 1619 helped to establish in America the idea that the colonies developing up and down the Atlantic seaboard ought to have some say in their own affairs, and not simply be ordered around by the government in London. A century and a half later the idea and practice of representative government would be so fully developed in America that perceived violations of it by the mother country could inspire a revolution.

There was more to Edwin Sandys's new plan for Virginia. For one, a lot of the harsh military laws were dropped. For another, people who paid their own way to America would automatically be granted fifty acres of land; and those who signed up indentured servants would also be given fifty acres for every servant sent.

The Virginia Assembly met for the first time on July 30, 1619. The session, held in Jamestown, lasted for only a few days, but over the next few years the legislature passed many important laws regulating trade with the Indians, requiring all planters to grow food as well as tobacco, reorganizing the company storehouse, and affecting many other matters.

Taken together, these changes helped to give Virginians a sense that the country was theirs—that they were not in the new land solely to make profits for somebody else. The changes worked. In 1619, twelve hundred

(above) Preparing food was a daily constant. Two women prepare fruit and vegetables for a meal.

(right) Cooking was done on open fires. Meat and vegetables were boiled in iron pots that hung from hooks above the fire. Bread and pies were baked in vessels by the fire, and other food was fried directly over it.

It was not all work, however. Here people make a Christmas wreath.

immigrants came to Virginia, increasing the colony's population by sixty percent. Altogether, thirty-five hundred people came to Virginia in the three years after 1619. Many of them were beggars from the country roads and city streets. Others were teenaged orphans shipped out forcibly as a way to find a use for them. But a good portion of the new immigrants were "choice men, born and bred up to labour and industry"—ordinary farm people looking for a chance to better their lives.

The problems in Virginia were finally being solved, but back home in

London they were growing worse. The investors had still not got their money back and were bickering about how to show a profit for themselves. They were also quarreling with the autocratic James I. The king was spending too much money on his court, and on foreign affairs, and was constantly looking for new ways to get more. He put in a law requiring all tobacco from English colonies in America to be shipped directly to England where it could be taxed, instead of to another country, for example Holland, where it might bring a higher price. By 1623, things were in disarray. Now the king decided simply to take the company over. In part this was to give him greater control for his own purposes. But his primary reason for stepping in was to remedy deplorable conditions in the colony—the problems with the Indians, the high rate of illness and death, the general state of disorganization.

The investors protested, as they would surely lose their investments now; and the colonists protested also, for they were afraid that the king would take away their precious House of Burgesses. But the king pushed the change through. And in 1624, the Virginia Company, a disaster from the start, was dissolved, and Virginia became a crown colony, part of the British system, much as Ireland was.

This was a very important change, for it meant that the colony would be governed directly by the king in his own best interests; and the king, as we have seen, was bent on extracting as much money from the colonies as he could.

Just as the Virginians feared, the House of Burgesses was scrapped. Even so, the king's officials in Virginia had sense enough to realize that they could not rule in some autocratic fashion over a people who had gotten used to a measure of control over their own affairs. They established the practice of calling annual informal "conventions" of elected delegates to "advise" them. The decisions of these conventions were not binding on the king's officials, but they usually took them into account.

In practice, then, the Virginians continued to have a voice in how their

A Christmas dance featuring the "Lord of Misrule."

lives were to be run through representative bodies. Finally, in 1639, King James' successor, Charles I, reestablished the House of Burgesses with the powers that it originally held. Representative government would be an institution cherished by Americans henceforth, something they would fight for when they felt it was threatened.

We should keep in mind, of course, that colonial Virginia was by no means a democracy in the modern sense. Only a minority had the vote:

women and blacks were excluded, of course. Only adult white males with a certain amount of property actually could vote.

Further limiting the extent of representation over the remaining years of the 1600s was the development in Virginia of a class of wealthy planters, lawyers, and land speculators, usually members of great families who frequently intermarried. Most of the important people in the House of Burgesses came from these wealthy families.

Nonetheless, they were *elected*, not appointed by the king or Parliament. That principle, once established, put America on the road to what became over a couple of centuries our modern democracy.

CHAPTER VI

Slavery Comes to Virginia

The year 1619 saw the first meeting of a representative body in colonial North America, the first small step on the road to our democratic government. The same year also saw another small event with momentous consequences: the importation into Virginia of twenty "Negars," who joined thirty-two who had arrived earlier that year, the first Africans in what would become the United States. The whole history of American slavery, and the rights of blacks in the United States, has always been a very emotional one. Probably no issue has caused so much confusion, heartache, pain, and bloodshed in America as the relationship between the black and white races. The great Civil War, in which some 600,000 young Americans died, was at bottom about whether the nation would tolerate slavery. And it began in 1619 in Virginia.

Slavery was hardly invented by Americans. About a third of the cultures studied by anthropologists have kept slaves in one fashion or another. The Spanish conquerors of Mexico and Central America enslaved Indians to work in the mines digging for gold and silver. European sailors and other travelers who fell into the hands of Arabs and Turks were frequently enslaved, and as we have seen, John Smith was briefly a slave to the Turks. Sometimes the Indians enslaved other Indians. Indeed, many of the tribes in West Africa, where most of the American blacks came from, kept slaves, many of whom they sold to Arab slavers who took them north in great slave caravans. And while it is certainly true that European slavers sometimes raided African villages for slaves, most of the slaves who were brought to the Americas were sold to Europeans by other Africans.

Slavery, thus, was no novelty when Europeans began their conquest of the Americas. Nobody was either surprised or alarmed that the Spanish and the Portuguese were enslaving the Indians they had conquered: Indian emperors in Mexico and Central America had enslaved other Indians to work the same mines, and the Spanish simply continued the practice.

But as the mines were exhausted, it became clear to the Spanish that they would have to find new sources of wealth in the Americas—cash crops like sugar, rice, indigo, tobacco and eventually cotton. Growing crops of these kinds required a great deal of hard work, hoeing away the weeds, killing bugs, turning cane into sugar, drying tobacco, and cleaning cotton.

The Indians, however, had the troublesome habit of dying quickly, partly due to the hard conditions of slavery, but mostly because of the diseases the Europeans brought with them. The supply of Indian slaves dwindled, and the Europeans turned to Africa as a source.

Some Europeans had been keeping African slaves even before Columbus sailed to America. For centuries there had been a certain number of slaves in Spain and Portugal, and in the 1400s the Portuguese, among the leading explorers of the time, started bringing home slaves from West Africa by the thousands.

Thus, keeping black slaves from Africa was something the Spanish and Portuguese were used to, and they simply continued the practice in the New World. By 1550, black slavery was a settled institution in the

Caribbean and in Central and South America. Other European nations building colonies in the Caribbean quickly adopted the practice, and by 1619, tens of thousands of Africans were being shipped across the Atlantic each year. The long ocean voyage was one of the worst aspects of slavery. The slaves were chained into cramped, stifling holds, often suffering from sickness, and eating the minimum amount of food and water. True, they were brought up on deck from time to time in order to give them air and sun for their health; in some cases slavers actually required them to sing and dance in the foolish hope that it would keep up their spirits. Thousands of slaves died on the trip. Others attempted to commit suicide, flinging themselves overboard if they had the chance, or clawing open their wrists with their fingernails. Most slaves arrived in the New World in abject misery.

Why did Virginians decide they needed to introduce this unhappy institution? The answer is simple: tobacco. In Virginia land was easy to get: the government was handing out fifty-acre chunks of land to anyone who could qualify, and on the frontier men were staking out large pieces on whatever excuse they could find. What was lacking in Virginia was labor. It was no use to hold a lot of land if you couldn't work it. At first landowners depended upon indentured servants, whom they sometimes bought and sold among themselves. These indentured servants were not exactly slaves, but they were not far from it. They could be whipped for small offenses, like talking back to a master. One master gave a girl, Alice Bennett, no less than five hundred lashes, and there were cases of servants being beaten to death, with the masters going unpunished. Servants were given the roughest kind of diets, at times just corn and water. They wore a minimum of clothing, and worked long hours. These servants did have some protections: a master could not simply abandon a servant before his term was up, and in some instances the master had to supply servants with provisions to get started with when they obtained their freedom.

This sort of harsh treatment of servants would not have been tolerat-

A reconstruction of a slave cabin of the 1700s, when slavery had become well established in Virginia. Note the fence woven of branches and saplings.

ed in England, where people generally hired out for only a year in any case. But in the primitive conditions of the settlements on the edge of a wilderness, people grew hard. By 1619, Virginians were already living with a system that was akin to slavery, differing in that indentured servants would eventually be free—though in the early years few of them lived to complete their term.

Nonetheless, Virginians were not quite ready to follow the course of their fellow colonists in the Caribbean Islands to the south. By 1650, there were only five hundred blacks in Virginia, compared to about fourteen thousand whites.

Part of the reason why Virginians did not take to black slavery more rapidly was because of the expense. The death rate in Virginia was high, especially among newcomers unused to the climate, the diseases, and the hardships of the new land. A high proportion of servants did not live out their terms of indenture. The price of a slave was roughly twice what it cost to bring over a servant; why buy an African for a lifetime that might prove to be quite short when you could get a European—whose life might be just as short—for half the price?

A second reason why slavery developed relatively slowly in Virginia was because the English—indeed Europeans in general—had mixed feelings about blacks. They seemed to the English not quite the same sort of people as themselves. According to the Bible, which their own King, James I, had recently had retranslated by scholars, blacks were in the eyes of God their equals, possessed of immortal souls, just like them. But they could also find in the same Bible justification for the slavery of blacks: hadn't Noah cursed Canaan, son of Ham, saying that he would be a "servant of servants," and wasn't Ham black?

In sum, Africans seemed to Europeans in general and English people in particular as not merely different, but inferior. The English were hardly alone in this belief: most peoples see themselves as superior to the other peoples around them. It seems to be a common way of thinking. The English vaguely felt that it was better not to associate with blacks. Very few blacks were ever brought into England, nor was slavery ever very important in the northern colonies developing along the Hudson and in New England, where there were few large-scale farms growing a cash

Interior of a slave cabin. Food was cooked over the fireplace in rough pots.

crop like sugar or tobacco. Though slavery was legal in the north and did exist in every colony there, northerners did not have a great need for slaves.

But the tobacco growers of Virginia did. In a place where land was plentiful, a simple equation held: labor equaled money. And so, somewhat reluctantly at first, the Virginians began to import Africans in ever-larger numbers.

Historians today argue over whether the first blacks in Virginia really were treated as slaves. Indeed, we are not sure that any of the first "twenty Negars" sold in Virginia by their Dutch captor were slaves; they may have been conventional servants. It appears that the Virginians themselves were not sure how they should be treated. Some were treated as slaves were in the Caribbean; some were treated as indentured servants and eventually given their freedom. In general, they were treated in the same way white servants were—that is, worked hard under harsh conditions, but not ground down as slaves were later on. One slave was able to earn enough money to buy his daughters out of slavery, and apprentice them to a master until they grew up. Others raised cattle, had their own farms, kept servants—even slaves—of their own. Some masters freed their slaves in their wills. Richard Vaughan said in his will that his black girls should be taught to read, given religious instruction, and when they grew up given clothes, blankets, cows and other provisions to get started with. But these were the exceptions.

About 1660, all this began to change. In that year the English people restored the king to the throne, ending twenty years of turmoil, including eleven of rule by Parliament without a king. There was less reason for people to emigrate. Further, as conditions in Virginia improved, indentured servants tended more frequently to live out their terms, at which time their masters usually had to provide them with tools, clothing and perhaps land. For a number of reasons, then, it began to make more sense to use slaves rather than servants; and fortuitously, at the same moment, the price for sugar from Barbados fell, creating a surplus of slaves there who could be bought for bargain prices.

So the use of slaves increased. As tobacco made at least some people wealthy, they bought more land, and brought in more slaves to work it. By the early part of the 1700s, more than half the workers in Virginia

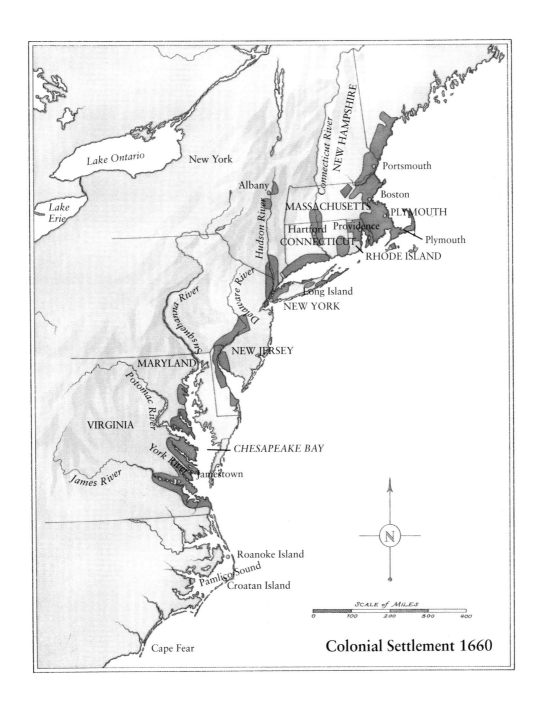

Colonial Settlement 1660

were black slaves. Rapidly thereafter, the institution of slavery became deeply embedded in the life of the colony.

The Virginia planters were now faced with one hard truth about slavery: the slaves did not like it. They would run away if they could, and thousands of them did. Furthermore, they had nothing whatsoever to gain by working hard, or working at all, for that matter. Somehow, they had to be made to work.

There was yet a further problem: as the number of slaves increased throughout the 1700s, whites in many places found themselves outnumbered by their slaves, in some cases by two or three times. The danger of a slave rebellion appeared to the whites very real. They had to assume that if the slaves rebelled, the masters and their families would be slaughtered from the outset. Whites in such situations lived in a permanent state of fear of their own captives.

Slaves had to be controlled. At the beginning, at least a few masters offered slaves rewards for working hard, such as promising them their freedom after a certain number of years in return for good behavior, or giving them small plots of land to raise tobacco on, which they could sell to make a little money of their own. But this was akin to turning slaves into indentured servants, and took the whole point out of slavery.

In the end, as slavery became a way of life in Virginia, the whites concluded that the only way to control their slaves was through punishment. Threaten them with the whip and they would behave. We do not have accurate figures on how often slaves were whipped, but it is probable that few slaves wholly escaped this punishment; and it is clear that rebellious or recalcitrant slaves were whipped every few days until they learned to obey. Thirty lashes was routine, and particularly difficult slaves were whipped until their backs were bloody and scarred forever.

Whipping, however, was not the only punishment. Slave owners were particularly hard on slaves who ran away. Such slaves might have their toes chopped off, for example. Slave owners of course did not want to

The life of the slaves was nearly constant work, especially during peak farm periods such as planting and harvesting times, when they might work on into night by moonlight. This reenactment shows a man hewing a beam for construction of a building. Some slaves were trained to do skilled tasks like this, but most spent their days in the fields, hoeing and picking.

Slaves usually, although not always, had Sundays free. They might tend small gardens of their own or enjoy music and dancing. Their music combined the European types of their masters with the kinds they had brought from Africa. In this reenactment, slaves are using gourd rattles and percussion instruments modeled on African ones.

maim their slaves, for that would have limited their usefulness, and they certainly didn't want to kill a slave worth several hundred dollars. But sometimes slaves died from vicious beatings, and there were laws saying that a master could not be charged with a crime if he killed a slave through harsh punishment. The law went even further: a runaway slave could be killed on the spot by anyone, and the government would reimburse his master for the loss, thus providing an incentive for murdering difficult or useless slaves. Needless to say, similar laws did not apply to white servants. In sum, slave owners believed, probably correctly, that they could keep their slaves in place only through the threat of very severe punishment.

We must keep it in mind that not all Virginia whites were vicious, and not all slave owners went out of their way to whip their slaves. To begin with, as slavery spread through the other southern colonies in the 1700s, the *majority* of whites did not own any slaves at all, and most of those who did owned only a few. The big plantations with hundreds of slaves laboring in the fields under the overseer's lash were relatively small in number. In the 1700s and early 1800s, most slaves lived on small farms, where black and white children grew up together playing in the dust before the cabin door. In these very common cases relationships between slaves' and the masters' family might be friendly.

Nonetheless, even where relationships were more friendly masters would at times beat their slaves. True, they beat white servants as well, but there was always a difference in the ways white servants and black slaves were treated. Perhaps the most inhumane practice was the breaking up of black families when a father or mother was sold away or children taken from parents; this would not be done to white servants. Even the kindest of masters felt that their slaves were an inferior kind of people who had to be dealt with firmly; and there were plenty of slave owners who felt no kindness towards their blacks at all.

Indeed, virtually all seventeenth-century Americans, even those who hated slavery, believed that blacks were inferior to whites. They were, in this view, childlike, or some lower order of humans, who had to be subjugated for their own good. This sort of racism existed everywhere, but in the South it was a central part of white mentality. Whites there *had* to believe it, otherwise slavery was impossible to justify. Even those southern whites who did not keep slaves believed in the inferiority of blacks as a matter of faith and principle. For the millions of poor whites in the South, it was important for them to feel that at least somebody was below them on the social scale.

The developing Virginia colony, thus, was living in the midst of a great paradox. On the one hand, through its legislative assembly, it was gradually leading the way towards greater equality and freedom for ordinary people. On the other hand, through the institution of slavery, it was binding millions of people into a system of oppression as bad as any the world has ever seen. It was a contradiction that could not endure, and in 1861, it exploded in the carnage of a great civil war.

BIBLIOGRAPHY

Many of the books that are no longer in print may still be found in school or public libraries.

For Students

Barden, Renardo. *The Discovery of America: Opposing Viewpoints*. San Diego: Greenhaven Press, 1989.

Calloway, Colin G. *Indians of the Northeast*. The First Americans Series. New York: Facts on File, 1991.

Gerson, Noel B. *Survival: Jamestown, First English Colony in America*. Parsippany, N.J.: Julian Messner, 1978. (Out of print.)

Hulton, Paul, ed. *America 1585: The Complete Drawings of John White*. Chapel Hill: University of North Carolina Press, 1984. (Out of print.)

Quiri, Patricia R. *The Algonquians*. Reprint. First Books. Danbury, Conn.: Franklin Watts, 1992.

Scott, John Anthony. *Settlers on the Eastern Shore: The British Colonies in North America, 1607 1750.* Library of American History Series. New York: Facts on File, 1991.

For Teachers

Axtell, James. *The European and the Indian: Essays in the Ethnohistory of Colonial North America.* New York: Oxford University Press, 1982.

Barbour, Philip L. *The Three Worlds of Captain John Smith.* Boston: Houghton Mifflin, 1964. (Out of print.)

Bridenbaugh, Carl. *Vexed and Troubled Englishmen, 1590-1642.* New York: Oxford University Press, 1968. (Out of print.)

Jennings, Francis. *The Invasion of America: Indians, Colonialism, and the Cant of Conquest.* Chapel Hill: University of North Carolina Press, 1975.

Kupperman, Karen Ordahl. *Roanoke: The Abandoned Colony.* Lanham, Md.: Rowman and Littlefield, 1984.

Morgan, Edmund S. *American Slavery-American Freedom: The Ordeal of Colonial Virginia.* New York: W. W. Norton, 1976.

Mossiker, Frances. *Pocahantas: The Life and the Legend.* New York: Alfred A. Knopf, 1976.

Rountree, Helen C. *Pocahontas's People: The Powhatan Indians of Virginia Through Four Centuries.* Norman, Okla.: University of Oklahoma Press, 1990.

_____. *The Powhatan Indians of Virginia: Their Traditional Culture.* Norman, Okla.: University of Oklahoma Press, 1989.

Tate, Thad W., and David L. Ammerman, eds. *The Chesapeake in the Seventeenth Century: Essays on Anglo-American Society.* Chapel Hill: University of North Carolina Press, 1979.

Trigger, Bruce G., ed. *Northeast.* Handbook of North American Indians Series. Vol. 15. Washington, D.C.: Smithsonian Institution Press, 1979.

Vaughan, Alden T. *American Genesis: Captain John Smith and the Founding of Virginia.* New York: Little, Brown, 1975.

INDEX

inhabitants, defined, 64–65
Ireland, 10, 14, 69
Italians, 14

James I, King (England)
    as James VI of Scotland, 70
    and King James Bible, 76
    Parliament and, 63
    Powhatan and, 46
    tobacco smoking disliked by, 54
    Virginia as crown colony under, 69
    Virginia's royal charter from, 42–43
James River, 44, 46, 53, 54, 59, 64
Jamestown colony
    Algonquian Indians and, 31
    colonists' arrival at, 43–44
    diseases in, 46, 47
    food shortages in, 49, 52–53
    fort, **46, 50, 51**
    legislative assembly meetings in, 66
    massacre of 1622, 59
    Powhatan and, 46–57
    in 1622, **52**
    Virginia Company and, 61–62, 66
Japan, 10
Jefferson, Thomas, 9
Jews, 14
joint stock companies, 60–61

King James Bible, 76
Kitty Hawk, 35
Kiwasa (Indian idol), **36**

land
    English system of ownership, 17–18, 20,
       24, 26
    farm laborers, **11**, 14, 68
    fifty acres to immigrants to Virginia, 66, 74
    Indian concept of, 32
    and unemployment in England, 21–22
    women and, 20

of yeomen, 17
language, 13, 31
law
    English, 13
    and representative government, 66
    and slaves, 83
    and tobacco tax, 69
liberty, personal, 15
literature, English, 12, 13–14
London. *See* England
Lord Governor, 62
Lost Colony of Roanoke, 35, 37, 40, 41, 42

Madison, James, 9
Magna Carta, 14–15, **15, 16**
Maine, 31, 43
malaria, 46
maps, 45, 79
Maryland, 61
Mason, George, 9
massacre of 1622, 59
measles, 33
Merchant of Venice, The, 13
Mexico, slavery in, 10, 72, 73
ministers (clergymen), 20
money economy, 24, 26
music
    English composers, 12
    slaves and, **82**

Native Americans. *See* Indians
Newfoundland, 28
New England, 76
New World. *See also* North America
    European colonization of, 10–20
    slavery in. *See* slavery
New York, 13
Newfoundland, 10, 28
Noah, 76
Norse explorers, 10
North America

JAMES LINCOLN COLLIER is the author of a number of books both for adults and for young people, including the social history *The Rise of Selfishness in America*. He is also noted for his biographies and historical studies in the field of jazz. Together with his brother, Christopher Collier, he has written a series of award-winning historical novels for children widely used in schools, including the Newbery Honor classic *My Brother Sam Is Dead*. A graduate of Hamilton College, he lives with his wife in New York City.

CHRISTOPHER COLLIER grew up in Fairfield County, Connecticut, and attended public schools there. He graduated from Clark University in Worcester, Massachusetts, and earned M.A. and Ph.D. degrees at Columbia University in New York City. After service in the Army and teaching in secondary schools for several years, Mr. Collier began teaching college in 1961. He is now Professor of History at the University of Connecticut and Connecticut State Historian. Mr. Collier has published many scholarly and popular books and articles about Connecticut and American history. With his brother, James, he is the author of nine historical novels for young adults, the best known of which is *My Brother Sam Is Dead*. He lives with his wife, Bonnie, a librarian, in Orange, Connecticut.